This book is dedicated to my children, Jordan and Makayla Crews. I want to leave a legacy for you. I want you to know that all things are possible, no matter what the odds are against you. You both will be successful and live amazing lives. I speak that over you now. I love you both!

Mommy

Table of Contents

_____

Introduction

At some point, we have to let go of the past, unhealthy relationships, baggage and all of the "Life Stuff" that is bombarding us on a daily basis and begin to walk in freedom! Freedom is a choice that you have to make for you! So many people never experience the feeling of really living, because they are side-tracked by the repetition of comfortable, chaos and confusion. They have grown so accustomed to dysfunction and have forgotten how to function effectively.

God does not want us to wait until perfect timing arrives to embrace His purpose for our lives. He wants us to walk in our now. Most often our destiny is birth out of a place of imperfection. Take a moment to think over the last ten years of your life. What if you would've maximized every moment and captured God opportunities that were presented to you? Where would you be right now? The good news is God is a redeemer of time and He wants you to prosper!

This book, while simplistic and practical, is written to challenge you. A good or bad habit is formed by doing the same thing for at least 28 days. I want God to shift your mindset. He wants you to experience the exceeding abundantly above all. We quote it and now it is time to live it. God wants to intricately detail every part of your promise and deliver it to you, but you have to desire it. You have to desire Him more than complacency.

I am challenging you to take your life back starting right now! Take responsibility and accountability for where you are. You have the power through Jesus Christ to do all things. This is according to His power that is working within us. I challenge you for to wake up, read, believe, apply and receive. Watch God release favor, blessing and increase into your life. Your explicit trust and faith in Him is provoking Him to move on your behalf right now. Watch for the manifestation of His promise to be revealed through you. It will happen, because you are choosing to **"Maximize Your Life!"**

Declaration One

"Let Go, Let God"

If you have ever stayed in any hotel, there will always be a laundry/dry-cleaning bag and laundry list hanging in the closet. Of course, this is for your convenience, but so many people are carrying around the laundry list of life with them every day. They keep it in their wallet, purse and pocket. This private list is a constant reminder of pain, issues, guilt and fear, past regrets, faults, rejection and offenses. Every time a new hurtful experience happens, it is just added to the laundry list. Before they know it, they have compiled years of painful memories and continue to remind themselves every time they look at the list. If you are going to maximize your life, you have to be willing to completely let go!

You can't take old issues into your now moment and season. You have to allow God to remove the build-up, callouses, residue and roots. There are some things you may never be able to change, but you can choose to give it to God. You know the several issues, thoughts or secrets that overwhelm you. For some people, this is happening on a daily basis. Today, I challenge you to rip up your laundry list!

Isaiah 43:18-19

Amplified Bible (AMP)

[18] Do not [earnestly] remember the former things; neither consider the things of old.

[19] Behold, I am doing a new thing! Now it springs forth; do you not perceive *and* know it *and* will you not give heed to it? I will even make a way in the wilderness and rivers in the desert.

Daily Decree

Today, I am choosing to let go of **everything** that I have been carrying for any amount of time. I am not going to dwell on past hurts. I want to experience the new thing and place that God has for me. I want to see it spring forth in my life. I will not go back to the old place again! I believe that I am free, in Jesus name.

I'm letting go of:

❖ _____

_____

_____

_____

_____

_____

Declaration Two

"Renew My Mind"

Our change and shift has to begin and remain in our mind. The enemy loves to use our mind as a battlefield. Most often, we are fighting unnecessary mental battles that handicap or cripple us. We are over-thinking and over-analyzing situations that we never had to waste time on. We are thinking about people, issues, relationships, jobs and the list could be endless. Many of the very things we are thinking about will never fit into God's plan for our lives. Your old ideals and attitudes are not applicable in this new time of your life, especially when you have chosen to let go! We have to continually renew our subscriptions to God on a daily basis. You have to be in a posture where you allow Him to reset and rewire your thinking! He only wants the best for you. He wants you to accelerate above a mediocre mindset. Mediocrity makes us lazy, because we never strive for more than the norm. Imagine what it would be like to walk in the perfect and acceptable will of God for your life!

You can do it, when you allow God to completely transform your mind! You have to allow Him total access. Start right now, by handing over everything that has weighed you down in your thinking. You will not be overwhelmed anymore. God is hitting control alt delete. He wants you to have a fresh start every day!

Romans 12:2

Amplified Bible (AMP)

2 Do not be conformed to this world (this age), [fashioned after and adapted to its external, superficial customs], but be transformed (changed) by the [entire] renewal of your mind [by its new ideals and its new attitude], so that you may prove [for yourselves] what is the good and acceptable and perfect will of God, *even* the thing which is good and acceptable and perfect [in His sight for you].

Daily Decree

I am giving God control of my mind, starting today! Lord, I want your perfect will for my life. I believe you are transforming my thoughts. Push the reset button on my mindset. Let me begin to think the way you want me to think!

Renew my mind concerning:

❖ _____

_____

_____

_____

_____

_____

Declaration Three

"Trust Issues"

Trust is a very delicate subject. So many people have been through painful situations that have completely annihilated the possibility of trusting again. This comes from betrayal, infidelity, gossip, broken confidence and no follow-through, just to name a few. It is easier to put up a wall and guard one's self instead of allowing people to have access. Because we don't want to suffer any more collateral damage, we will tend to isolate ourselves. Let's start by acknowledging that "trust issues" do not just happen, but are actually *created* by the events that have occurred in a person's life. Getting rid of "trust issues" takes time and diligence, but it certainly can be done! It's important to know that healing occurs at the same place that the injury itself occurred. In other words, in order to start healing your "trust issues" you must first know when, where, and by whom your trust was breeched. After doing your self-reflection, decide to forgive the people who've hurt you and have likely contributed to your issues with trust. Remember, forgiving is for you, NOT for the other person.

When you're able to forgive someone who's wronged you, you're finally able to release all of the negativity that has been pent up inside of you. We have to learn how put our complete trust in God! God is not like man! That doesn't mean it will necessarily be easy for us to trust God, but it does mean that we should try not to allow human failings to rob us of the comfort of God's dependability. Sometimes we need to pray, like the man in Mark's gospel who was let down by Jesus' disciples and so struggled to trust Jesus himself: He said, "I believe; help my unbelief!" Allowing yourself to trust someone requires you to open up your inner world to that person. This can be really hard, especially if you've been burned in the past. However, you deserve GREAT relationships in any capacity. Choose to allow The Holy Spirit to guide you and your relationships will soon begin to bear fruit.

Proverbs 3:5-6

Amplified Bible (AMP)

[5] Lean on, trust in, *and* be confident in the Lord with all your heart *and* mind and do not rely on your own insight *or* understanding.

[6] In all your ways know, recognize, *and* acknowledge Him, and He will direct *and* make straight *and* plain your paths.

Daily Decree

Dear God, thank you for your love. I want you to remove any blockage in my heart. I will trust you first! I will lean and rely on you and not my emotions. I will allow myself to forgive. I want and desire your direction in my life. Please regulate my heart and mind. I believe in your infinite wisdom.

I will trust you with:

❖ _____

_____

_____

_____

_____

_____

Declaration Four

"No Response Necessary"

When you choose to be focused, it seems like that is when people can be at their worst. It is unfortunate that some people secretly do not want you to succeed. The easiest way to distract us is with words that hurt. This often triggers our emotions to go into a frenzy and ignites a reaction. Can you shift your emotional state at will? Most of us can't. When, we get emotionally triggered we're toast. We want to retreat or react. Our brain has left the proverbial safety station and we're on it. We're stuck. We're stressed. We are reacting instead of responding, IF we choose to. Performance, promise and purpose hijackers are people who are jealous, intimidated and manipulative. They often know the exact buttons to push. You are responsible for identifying your adversary. Stop giving them the satisfaction of your reaction. Your mandate is to continue working, focusing, purposing, finishing and exceling. You need to consider new behaviors that confuse and cancel the assignment of your critics. You are already declared a winner, so stay FOCUSED!

Nehemiah 6

Amplified Bible (AMP)

6 Now when Sanballat, Tobiah, Geshem the Arab, and the rest of our enemies heard that I had built the wall and that there was no breach left in it, although at that time I had not set up the doors in the gates,

2 Sanballat and Geshem sent to me, saying, Come, let us meet together in one of the villages in the plain of Ono. But they intended to do me harm.

3 And I sent messengers to them, saying, I am doing a great work and cannot come down. Why should the work stop while I leave to come down to you?

4 They sent to me four times this way, and I answered them as before.

5 Then Sanballat sent his servant to me again the fifth time with an open letter.

6 In it was written: It is reported among the neighboring nations, and Gashmu says it, that you and the Jews plan to rebel; therefore you are building the wall, that you may be their king, according to the report.

7 Also you have set up prophets to announce concerning you in Jerusalem, There is a king in Judah. And now this will be reported to the

[Persian] king. So, come now and let us take counsel together.

[8] I replied to him, No such things as you say have been done; you are inventing them out of your own heart *and* mind.

[9] For they all wanted to frighten us, thinking, Their hands will be so weak that the work will not be done. But now strengthen my hands!

[10] I went into the house of Shemaiah son of Delaiah, the son of Mehetabel, who was shut up. He said, Let us meet together in the house of God, within the temple, and let us shut the doors of the temple, for they are coming to kill you—at night they are coming to kill you.

[11] But I said, Should such a man as I flee? And what man such as I could go into the temple [where only the priests are allowed to go] and yet live? I will not go in.

[12] And behold, I saw that God had not sent him, but he made this prophecy against me because Tobiah and Sanballat had hired him.

[13] He was hired that I should be made afraid and do as he said and sin, that they might have matter for an evil report with which to taunt *and* reproach me.

[14] My God, think on Tobiah and Sanballat according to these their works, and on the prophetess Noadiah and the rest of the prophets who would have put me in fear.

[15] So the wall was finished on the twenty-fifth day of the month Elul, in fifty-two days.

[16] When all our enemies heard of it, all the nations around us feared and fell far in their own esteem, for they saw that this work was done by our God.

Daily Decree

I will no longer react. I will only respond if it is necessary and God-directed. I will stay focused and allow God to be in control of my emotions. I will finish strong!

I will no longer react to:

❖ _____

_____

_____

_____

_____

Declaration Five

"Don't Give Up"

Some days do you just want to quit? Perhaps, you are tired of trying and, in all probability, you're spinning your wheels and getting nowhere. You may see other people less deserving getting ahead, and you are stuck in the same place. Life might have gotten monotonous. Feelings of inadequacy seep into your mind. Or, a setback has caused you to fall back into old, destructive patterns. Now, you could be off-track, discouraged and your energy may be drained. But wait. You count. Your life matters. No matter what you are going through today, God has not given up on you, so don't give up on yourself. Decide now to get off the treadmill of negative thoughts and see beyond the present moment. God has a wonderful plan and place for you. And your future holds great promise. Your life is full of countless possibilities. You have too much yet to do, too many lives to positively influence and too many dreams to make manifest to quit now. Your time for victory, too, is coming. So, whatever may be troubling you, turn it all over to God and progress ahead. There is no obstacle too big for God to turn around for your greater good.

Galatians 6:9

Amplified Bible (AMP)

[9] And let us not lose heart *and* grow weary *and* faint in acting nobly *and* doing right, for in due time *and* at the appointed season we shall reap, if we do not loosen *and* relax our courage *and* faint.

Daily Decree

I will not give up! I know that my season is here. In, fact I am going to speak to my right now. I will reap a harvest! Dear God, I will continue to believe in my promise. Your promise for me is guaranteed. So, no matter what it looks like, I am going to keep moving forward. I repeat, I will not give up. I know you are able to do exceeding abundantly above all in my life! Thank you in advance for the victory.

I am believing God regardless of:

❖ _____

_____

_____

Declaration Six

"Big Plans"

God gives us hopes and dreams for certain things to happen in our lives, but He doesn't always allow us to see the exact timing of His plan. Although frustrating, not knowing the exact timing is often what keeps us in the program. There are times when we might give up if we knew how long it was going to take, but when we accept God's timing, we can learn to live in hope and enjoy our lives while God is working on our problems. We know that God's plan for our lives is good, and when we entrust ourselves to Him, we can experience total peace and happiness. Sometimes it can be so hard, because we have so many questions! Who should I marry? Should I go back to school? Is this the place where God wants me to serve? Should I start my own business? Are my children going to be ok? When should I buy a home? When should I retire? Where is God calling me? Is this job a dead-end? What's the next step in my life? Which church should I attend? Am I really on track with God's will for my life? We have to know and trust two distinct things. Isn't it good that God knows the plans He has for us? Sometimes, we would wish that we also might be allowed to

23

know. But whether we know or not, God knows. God's plans are good and not harmful and they to give us hope and an expected end. God has amazing plans for your life. He knows everything about you. He made you and He loves you!

Jeremiah 29:11

Amplified Bible (AMP)

[11] For I know the thoughts *and* plans that I have for you, says the Lord, thoughts *and* plans for welfare *and* peace and not for evil, to give you hope in your final outcome.

Daily Decree

Dear God, I am going to trust in the plans you have concerning my life! I know that you only want the best for me. I will rest in your will! I am going to wait on the tailor-made promise that you are designing for me. Your plans are perfect for me.

The promises God made me are:

❖ _____

_____

_____

_____

_____

_____

_____

_____

Declaration Seven

"The Waiting Room"

Waiting is so hard! We wait in line at the department store, the ER, restaurants and auto shops and on top of that we have to wait on God! We spend a lot of time in our lives waiting, because change is a process. Many people want change, but they don't want to go through the waiting process. But the truth is, waiting is a given—we are going to have to wait. You heard from God, but nothing happened or is happening yet. You've read your Bible and underlined the right verses, but the reality of the wait is crushing you. You've waited so long, you're beginning to wonder if God is mad at you or if you offended Him in some way. You're thinking, if you just do the right things or pray the right mix of words, somehow God will notice you—because He hasn't seemed to notice you yet. You say, "God do you see me in this situation?" But, we have to remember, God is preparing you for a successful transition into His plan. He has the perfect time and wants to make sure you are ready to receive it or vice-versa! If He does it too soon, you won't be ready for it and it won't be ready for you. Don't confuse times of waiting as a sign of God's anger. You're going through a process that prepares you for the plans God has for you. He is only refining you. The timing of your official release will be perfect. The question is, are we going to wait the wrong or right way? If we wait the wrong way, we'll be miserable; but if we decide to wait God's way, we can become patient and enjoy the wait. It takes practice, but as we let God help us in each situation, we develop patience. You can rest in knowing that it will be worth the wait!

Isaiah 40:31

Amplified Bible (AMP)

³¹ But those who wait for the Lord [who expect, look for, and hope in Him] shall change *and* renew their strength *and* power; they shall lift their wings *and* mount up [close to God] as eagles [mount up to the sun]; they shall run and not be weary, they shall walk and not faint *or* become tired.

Daily Decree

Dear God, I am willing to wait on you. I know your will is perfect for me. In my waiting, I will allow you to renew my strength. I will allow myself to learn the art of being patient and know that your infinite wisdom is working for me. I will expect, look for, hope and trust in you. I will not grow weary during this time, but instead focus on my future.

During my time of waiting, I will focus on:

❖ _____

_____

_____

_____

_____

_____

Declaration Eight

"Rejection is God's protection"

Rejection can be so hurtful to the point many people are handicapped by the feeling of someone not loving or accepting them. Rejection doesn't feel good and sometimes it feels unfathomable, but it shouldn't be something you permit to take away happiness from your life. Any kind of rejection, no matter if it's in love, your career, friends, a book proposal or anything else, is not something that should affect how happy you are. The suffering that happens when rejection occurs comes from over-thinking the "loss" that you feel you're suffering, be it loss of an opportunity, loss of a special relationship or loss of some other kind. The reality of life is that rejection will form a part of it—there will be occasions when your job application, your date request or your ideas for change will be rejected by someone, somewhere. For many of us, asking others for what we want scares the wits out of us, because it forces us out of the box of our comfort zone (that imaginary place where we have some illusionary semblance of being in control), and into the realm of uncertainty -- where we are absolutely out of control and thus, subject to the possibility of rejection. Let's face it, nobody likes to be told "no." As a result, and because the fear of rejection is so strong, there is a tendency for some of us is to sit back, lay low, stay quiet and thus, stay stuck in the box. The key is to remember if we don't ask, the answer will *always* be an automatic no. It is normal to feel bad, so don't try to bottle up your disappointment and sadness. However, don't allow yourself to feel this way for too long—you risk coloring your future endeavors with a negative impression if you start seeing this as something that will happen again, no matter what you do. You still have control, you still have an opportunity to learn from this experience and to approach the future wiser and more fortified. It is a healthy attitude to accept that rejection is a part of life and to acknowledge that what really matters is finding the way to bounce back and try again.

Romans 8:31

Amplified Bible (AMP)

[31] What then shall we say to [all] this? If God is for us, who [can be] against us? [Who can be our foe, if God is on our side?]

Daily Decree

Dear God, allow me to come to the place where I realize that most rejection is just your divine plan of protection. I am going settle my heart and mind. I am not going to be angry or broken from the experience of rejection, but instead, I will move forward. If you are for me, no one can be against me. I will allow you to define my worth. I will identify myself according to your word and thoughts towards me. I will no longer hope for their approval. I will accept the no. I know that behind the no is a greater place. The place that you have promised me a yes.

I will no longer suffer from rejection due to:

❖ _____

_____

_____

_____

_____

_____

Declaration Nine

"Guard Your Heart"

Because, it is in our nature to be loving and giving, we often forget to guard the most important thing in our lives, our heart. Many times we open up to people, because of their words. We form a relationship, before we have tested their words to see if they are valid. Why do we do this over and over again? We have to learn to weigh words with action. If the words are contradictory to the action, then we have to be discerning enough recognize and refuse to repeat the history lesson we already know too well. King Solomon said it best: "Above all else, guard your heart, for it is the wellspring of life" (Proverbs 4:23). He says it is the "wellspring of life." In other words, it is the source of everything else in your life. Your heart overflows into thoughts, words, and actions. This is why Solomon says, "Above all else." He doesn't say, "If you get around to it" or "It would be nice if." No, he says, *make it your top priority*. It is the essence of who you are. It is your authentic self—the *core* of your being. It is where all your dreams, your desires, and your passions live. It is that part of you that connects with God and other people. Your heart is priceless. You can't handle it haphazardly or allow others to have access to it that will not handle with care. We don't have to guard worthless things. I take my garbage to the street every Wednesday night. It is picked up on Thursday morning. It sits on the sidewalk all night, completely unguarded. Why? Because it is worthless. But, you would never do this with your heart. By giving toxic and damaging people or situations access to you, this is exactly what you are doing. If your heart is unhealthy, it has an impact on everything else. It threatens your family, your friends, your ministry, your career, and, indeed, your legacy. It is, therefore, imperative that you guard it. Your days of being heartbroken are officially over!

Proverbs 4:23

Amplified Bible (AMP)

[23] **Keep** *and* **guard your heart with all vigilance** *and* **above all that you guard, for out of it flow the springs of life.**

Daily Decree

Dear Lord, thank you for giving me wisdom in all my relationships. I want to be able to discern motives better than I have before. I want to have a healthy heart. I want to be in your will, concerning my connections. Allow me to see with spiritual vision and not my emotions.

I will guard my heart from:

❖ _____

_____

_____

_____

_____

_____

_____

Declaration Ten

"I'm God's Masterpiece"

A Masterpiece in modern usage refers to a creation that has been given much critical praise, especially one that is considered the greatest work of a person's career or to a work of outstanding creativity, skill, or workmanship. You have been personally created by the Master artist. He has hand-crafted you. None of His designs are the same. You are unique in every way. When God molded and made you, He tailor-made every detail about you. In God's eyes you are not monochrome! You are multi-faceted, vibrant and full of life and promise. You are His extraordinary billboard in the earth. He looks at you proudly and says, "I made her/him." He created you in His image and called it good. God has taken time to pay attention to the smallest detail that we often overlook about ourselves. When you are a masterpiece, you hold a very high value.

Many masterpieces are priceless. Ask God to allow you to see who you are through His eyes. He is your appraiser. We have to stop allowing people to define or assess our value, when they can't see our worth. You are an invaluable asset to God. He has hand-stamped you approved and authenticated. When you know you're priceless in Christ, you no longer have to prove your worth to people. Take a moment to write down 5-10 adjectives that perfectly describe you. This will not include your title. A masterpiece can never decrease in value. It only appreciates, even when it is flawed. You are God's masterpiece.

Psalm 139:14

King James Version (KJV)

[14] I will praise thee; for I am fearfully and wonderfully made: marvellous are thy works; and that my soul knoweth right well.

Daily Decree

Lord, help me to see myself through your eyes.
You never see me as man does.
Thank you for always viewing me as an asset and
never a liability. Thank you for approving and
appraising me as invaluable. I will no longer wait
for man to validate me. I am a masterpiece,
because God created me!

I am a masterpiece because:

❖ _____

_____

_____

_____

_____

_____

_____

_____

Declaration Eleven

"I Need a Breakthrough"

When you have gone through season after season of loss, lack, brokenness, breakdown and barrenness, you can start to lose your expectation for breakthrough. David ended up in this place in 1 Samuel 27, when he was being pursued by Saul. He got so tired that he went into the land of the Philistines and made covenant with King Achish. He was so overwhelmed with life that he forgot about his promise from God. Have you ever been there? David could run, but he could not hide. He was weary and worn out. There seemed to be no end to his troubles. The songs that are assigned to this period of David's life are sad songs. The overriding mood is one of dreary depression and despair. Why, O LORD, do you stand far off? Why do you hide yourself in times of trouble? (Psalm 10:1). How long, O LORD? Will you forget me forever? How long will you hide your face from me? (Psalm 13:1). My God, my God, why have you forsaken me? Why are you so far from saving me, so far from the words of my groaning? (Psalm 22:1). David had reached the end of his rope. He just couldn't take it anymore. He figured, if I go and hide and escape my enemy, he will despair looking for me. But, in order for him to get to breakthrough, he had to reposition himself in front of his promise and remember who he was. Breakthrough is defined as a sudden increase in knowledge and understanding or an important discovery that happens after trying for a long time to understand or explain something. Also, it carries this powerful definition which is most applicable to you. Breakthrough is an offensive thrust that penetrates and carries beyond a defensive line in warfare or an act or instance of breaking through an obstacle. You already have the promise. You just have to keep your focus, no matter what! When David got to Ziklag, where he was never supposed to be, he postured himself in prayer and sought a word from the Lord. He remembered how he won in the past. The word to him was to pursue and without fail he would recover it all. Don't stop pushing your way through every obstacle! Your breakthrough depends on your tenacity to win. Keep your eyes on the prize! You will win!

1 Samuel 30:8

Amplified Bible (AMP)

[8] And David inquired of the Lord, saying, Shall I pursue this troop? Shall I overtake them? The Lord answered him, Pursue, for you shall surely overtake them and without fail recover all.

Daily Decree

I am making up my mind to win, no matter what. I am going to stand! I am going to remind myself of your promises, God. I trust your plan for my life. I am not going to take any more detours. I am not going to allow my frustration to make me forfeit my blessings! I will walk in my place of total breakthrough!

I will have my breakthrough in these areas of my life:

❖ _____

_____

_____

_____

_____

_____

_____

Declaration Twelve

"Say Yes To Your Set-up"

So many of us have had to struggle for so long that we are unaccustomed with the place of blessing. Because we acclimate ourselves to lack, we become infatuated with insufficiency, inadequacy, insecurity and instability. It would not be a life choice, but many people are just simply used to this environment. When a person has heard "no" over and over, they program their mind to always receive a "no." Take Mephibosheth, in the Bible, for example. After he was dropped and crippled at five years old, he was placed in Lodebar. Lodebar was a place of no pasture, greenery or water. It was a dry and barren land. If you are used to a particular life landscape, it is hard to accept new scenery. We have to learn how to say "yes." God wants to bless us. He has portions set aside for us that have our name attached to them. When King David said, "Is there anyone left in the house of Saul that I may bless for Jonathan's sake?" The servant said, "Yes, Mephibosheth!" He was not forgotten.

After all the years and the waiting, what belonged to him was still his. Nobody can revoke what belongs to you, when God has reserved it for you. You just have to learn how to receive it! Mephibosheth said to David, "Why would you choose a dog such as I?" Don't dismiss your set-up by discounting yourself! Just learn how to say "yes" and "thank you!" Allow God to shift your mindset.

2 Samuel 9:7

Amplified Bible (AMP)

[7] David said to him, Fear not, for I will surely show you kindness for Jonathan your father's sake, and will restore to you all the land of Saul your father [grandfather], and you shall eat at my table always.

Daily Decree

Dear Lord, help me learn how to receive. I don't want to miss the blessings you have for me. I will say "yes" to your set-up for my life! I believe in restoration and overflow. I believe that my life can be easy. I will not struggle anymore! Release me from Lodebar and settle me in my set-up.

I will say yes and thank you to my set-up:

❖ _____

_____

_____

_____

_____

_____

_____

_____

Declaration

Thirteen

"I'm a Mountain Mover"

Let's do a faith check! Where does your level of faith lie? The definition of faith is complete trust or confidence in. Jesus says, "Have complete trust and relying fully on me." You have to have the God-kind of faith. The moment you were born again, you received "...a measure of faith" (Rom. 12:3). In other places Jesus referred to faith as "a mustard seed." (Matt. 17:20.) The faith you have now is capable of moving any mountain in your life. The "God-kind" of faith resides in you now. Jesus said, "...Whoever says to this mountain...." This means you are included since you are a "whoever." You can speak directly to the mountain and address it with authority. If the mountain is strife in the home or business, say, "Strife, in the name of Jesus, I command you to leave this place now." Then lift your hands and begin to thank God for removing the problem, or the mountain. When you know your authority, you will believe that what you say will come to pass. You have this assurance because Jesus regained authority over the devil through His death and resurrection. (Matt. 28:18-20.) You expect your words to be fulfilled because of your covenant with God. Doubt has no place in you, for faith has flooded your heart. You were born again to rule and reign in this earth under the authority of Jesus Christ. (Rom. 5:17.) Expect things to change as you speak, for God has given you the power to move mountains.

Mark 11:22-23

Amplified Bible (AMP)

[22] And Jesus, replying, said to them, Have faith in God [constantly].

[23] Truly I tell you, whoever says to this mountain, Be lifted up and thrown into the sea! and does not doubt at all in his heart but believes that what he says will take place, it will be done for him.

Daily Decree

I will speak to every mountain in my life. It will be removed, because I believe what I speak will be done. I have authority through Christ! Dear God, elevate my faith level to a new dimension. I will fully rely and completely trust in you.

I will move these mountains in my life:

❖ _____

_____

_____

_____

_____

_____

_____

_____

Declaration

Fourteen

"Forgiveness Equals Freedom"

Learning how to forgive others is one of the most unnatural duties in the Christian life. It goes against our human nature. Forgiving is a supernatural act that Jesus Christ was capable of, but when we are hurt by someone, we want to hold a grudge. We want justice. Sadly, we don't trust God with that. There is a secret to successfully living the Christian life, however, and that same secret applies when we're struggling with how to forgive. Jesus understood the brokenness of the human condition. No one knows the human heart like him. He forgave tax collectors and unlikely candidates and forgave Peter, for betraying him. On the cross, he even forgave the people who killed him. He knows that humans—all humans—are weak. For us, though, it usually doesn't help to know that those who have hurt us are weak. All we know is that we were injured and we can't seem to get over it. Jesus' command in the Lord's Prayer seems too hard to obey: "*And forgive us our debts, as we also have forgiven our debtors.*" (Mark 6:12, NIV) Refusing to forgive leaves an open wound in our soul that festers into bitterness, resentment, and depression. For our own good, and the good of the person who hurt us, we simply must forgive. Just as we trust God for our salvation, we have to trust him to make things right when we forgive. He will heal our wound so we can move on. Who are you helping most when you forgive the person who hurt you? Actually, you're helping yourself more than the other person. I always looked at forgiving people who hurt me as being really hard. I thought it seemed so unfair for them to receive forgiveness, when I had gotten hurt. I got pain, and they got freedom without having to pay for the pain they caused. Now I realize that I'm helping myself, when I choose to forgive. True forgiveness really does equal freedom.

Matthew 6:14

Amplified Bible (AMP)

[14] For if you forgive people their trespasses [their [a]reckless and willful sins, [b]leaving them, letting them go, and [c]giving up resentment], your heavenly Father will also forgive you.

Daily Decree

I am willing to let go of all the hurtful things that have been done to me. I am not going harbor any more pain. I am going to allow God to remove painful words from my heart, mind and spirit. I want to live in total freedom. I choose to forgive, even if it has to be between me and God. I forgive you.

I Choose to Forgive:

❖ _____

_____

_____

_____

_____

_____

_____

_____

Declaration Fifteen

"Bless Me Indeed"

To "bless" in the meaning of the Bible terms is a supernatural favor. It is not to ask for what we could get for ourselves, as far as houses, cars and things. It is to ask for God's goodness to be given to us, not someone else. It is leaving it entirely up to God to decide what the blessings will be, where, when and how He will bless us. To ask for God's blessings is to throw one's self entirely into the will of God and His power and purpose for our lives. It is becoming entirely involved in what God wants to do in us, through us, and around us all for His glory. What could we lose by not asking God's blessings to be upon us? We would lose that which we fail to ask for. Jesus said, **"Ask, and it will be given to you..."** James said, **"You do not have because you do not ask..."** It is the nature of God to bless and His blessings on us are limited by US, not by God nor His resources, or power or anything else. We limit God by our failure to ask. Do you think God has more for you than what you are experiencing? Then, ask God to enlarge your life, so you can in turn do more for Him. Ask for more influence, more responsibility, more opportunity, more service and more ability. Ask for more in order to bring more honor and glory to God, but not to or for yourself. Most of us think that we have too much already, but when we pray this prayer of asking God to increase, enlarge our life of service, amazing things can begin to happen-opportunities expand, ability and resources increase, doors are opened, new people come into your life and more unexpected things happen. Are you ready to be blessed indeed?

1 Chronicles 4:9-10

Amplified Bible (AMP)

[9] Jabez was honorable above his brothers; but his mother named him Jabez [sorrow maker], saying, Because I bore him in pain.

[10] Jabez cried to the God of Israel, saying, Oh, that You would bless me and enlarge my border, and that Your hand might be with me, and You would keep me from evil so it might not hurt me! And God granted his request.

DAILY DECREE

I believe that I will be blessed indeed! The blessings of the Lord maketh rich and never add sorrow or more pain. Dear Lord, keep your hand on me and pour your wisdom into me! I only want your will for my life. I know your will is a safe place for me. I believe in your blessings and promises for my life. I trust and love you God!

Bless me indeed in these areas:

❖ _____

_____

_____

_____

_____

_____

_____

_____

_____

_____

Contact Information

www.kellycrews.org

To contact or book Kelly Crews you may:

Email to:
kellycrewsministries@yahoo.com

Phone: 877.278.5975

Twitter: @prophetesskelly

Facebook: You may find her at her public figure page: "Kelly Crews"

Instagram: Kelly Crews

26962155R00032

Made in the USA
Charleston, SC
25 February 2014